IDEA LAB

Niki Ahrens

Lerner Publications ◆ Minneapolis

To the Linda Vista Library staff, who set an inspiring bar
for building and supporting community

Lerner Publications Company
A division of Lerner Publishing Group, Inc.
241 First Avenue North
Minneapolis, MN 55401 USA

For reading levels and more information, look up this title at www.lernerbooks.com.

Main body text set in Mikado a 14/18.
Typeface provided by HVD Fonts.

Library of Congress Cataloging-in-Publication Data

Names: Ahrens, Niki, 1979– author.
Title: Aladdin idea lab / Niki Ahrens.
Description: Minneapolis : Lerner Publications Minneapolis, [2020] | Series:
    Disney STEAM projects | Audience: Age 7–11. | Audience: Grade 4 to 6. | Includes
    bibliographical references and index.
Identifiers: LCCN 2018054303 (print) | LCCN 2018055352
    (ebook) | ISBN 9781541561540 (eb pdf) | ISBN 9781541554832 (lib. : alk. paper) |
    ISBN 9781541574007 (pbk. : alk. paper)
Subjects: LCSH: Handicraft—Juvenile literature. | Science projects—Juvenile
    literature. | Aladdin (Motion picture)—Juvenile literature. | Middle East—Social life
    and customs—Juvenile literature.
Classification: LCC TT160 (ebook) | LCC TT160 .A327 2020 (print) | DDC 745.5—dc23

LC record available at https://lccn.loc.gov/2018054303

Manufactured in the United States of America
1-45801-42683-3/26/2019

Contents

ONONDAGA FREE

STEAM Adventures with *Aladdin*

Aladdin and Jasmine dreamed of exploring the world and changing their lives. They set off on an enchanted adventure. They rode a magic carpet, befriended Genie, defeated an evil sorcerer, and much more.

Follow Jasmine and Aladdin's adventures in Agrabah, and learn about their world with science, technology, engineering, art, and math projects.

Before You Get Started

Each project includes a list of the materials you'll need. Gather them before you start. An adult can help you find the materials around your home, at a hardware or craft store, or online.

Choose a safe workspace, and cover it with newspaper or cardboard. This will make it easier to clean up when you're finished. Ask an adult for permission and help to use sharp tools and chemicals such as hydrogen peroxide.

Aladdin Zip Line

Aladdin slides down a clothesline to escape the palace guards. Make a zip line to send Aladdin zooming to lower ground.

Materials

- school glue
- 5 small leaves
- 1 large leaf
- 4 clothespins (optional)
- black marker
- 2 paper clips
- scissors
- string
- ruler
- countertop
- masking tape

1. Glue a small leaf to the top of the large leaf to form Aladdin's head and body. Then glue two leaf arms and two leaf legs to the body. You can use clothespins to hold the leaves together as the glue dries. When the glue is dry, remove the clothespins.

2. Draw a face on your leafy Aladdin. Attach a paper clip to the top of his head.

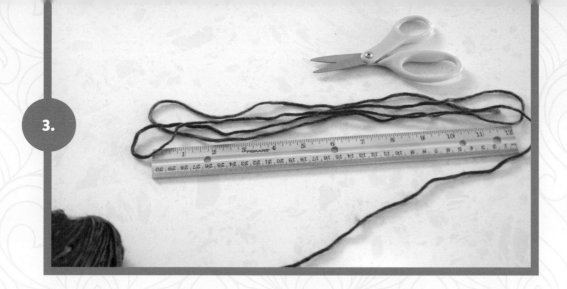

3. Cut a piece of string about 48 inches (122 cm) long.

4. Tape one end of the string to a countertop. Stretch the other end of the string away from the countertop in a slanting line to the floor. Make sure the string is pulled tight, and tape it to the floor.

5. Hook the second paper clip to the paper clip on Aladdin's head.

6. Hang Aladdin near the top of the string using the second paper clip. Let go of the paper clip to send him down the zip line to the floor. Try moving the taped string on the floor to see how different angles affect Aladdin's trip down the line.

STEAM Takeaway

Zip lines work because of Earth's gravity. Gravity is a force that pulls objects toward Earth's center. Gravity pulls on people on zip lines. It tugs them down the line toward the ground.

Blue Diamond

Jafar wants to capture the power of the Sultan's mystic blue diamond. Design a blue diamond to shine in your window.

Materials

- coffee filter
- blue marker
- water
- spray bottle
- scissors
- empty cereal box
- ruler
- pencil or pen
- black crayon or black paint
- clear tape

1.

1. Decorate a coffee filter with the blue marker.

2. Lightly spray the decorated coffee filter 1 to 3 times with water from the spray bottle. The water will cause the marker decorations to spread. Allow the coffee filter to dry.

3. Cut off the back of the cereal box. Fold the cut-off piece in half from top to bottom, keeping the plain side of the cardboard on the outside.

4. On one side of the folded cardboard, use the ruler to draw two lines, one from each end of the fold line. The lines should meet at the center of the opposite side. Cut along the lines to create a triangle shape.

5. Beginning about 1 inch (2.5 cm) from one end of the triangle's fold line, draw a line to the top center of the triangle. Do the same on the other side, and cut along the lines. Remove the small triangle, and set it aside.

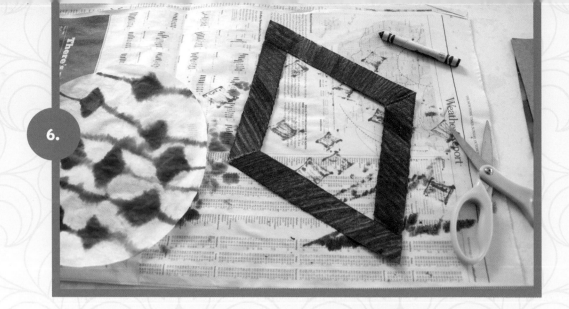

6. Unfold the larger piece into a diamond frame. Color the plain side of the cardboard with black crayon or black paint. If you use paint, let it dry.

7. Fit the blue coffee filter behind the diamond frame. Tape the top and bottom of the filter to the frame. Trim any filter that sticks out from the edges of the frame.

8. Add more tape to the coffee filter to secure it to the back of the frame. Display your blue diamond art against a window and let it shine!

Escape the Palace

Jasmine escapes the palace by climbing over a wall. You can build a machine to help reach the top of a wall.

Materials
- scissors
- empty tissue box
- ruler
- string
- clear tape
- unsharpened pencil
- paper clip
- bendy straw

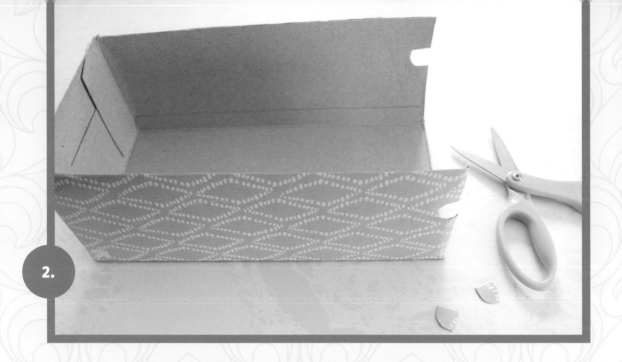

1. Cut off one end and the top of the tissue box.

2. Cut notches about 1 inch (2.5 cm) deep at the open end of the box on the left and right sides. The two notches should be across from each other and the right size to hold a pencil.

3. Cut an 18-inch-long (45 cm) string. Tape one end of the string to the center of the pencil. Tie a paper clip to the other end of the string.

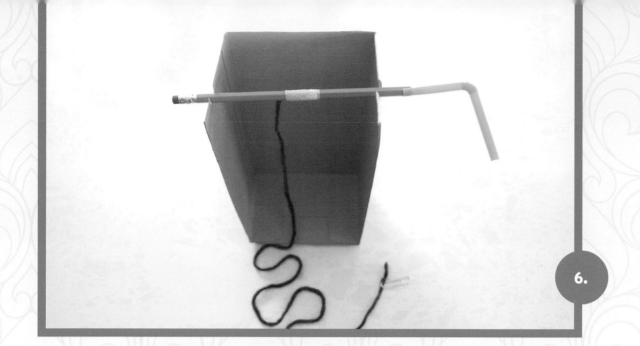

6.

4. Cut the straw in half. Discard the side without the bend. Insert the pencil into one end of the bendy straw piece. To help the pencil fit, you can widen the straw by cutting two tiny slits at the bottom.

5. Stand the box up with the open end facing up. Place the pencil across the top of the box in the notches. The eraser end and the straw end will stick out from the box.

6. Bend the straw to a right angle to make a crank. Reel up the paper clip by turning the bendy-straw crank.

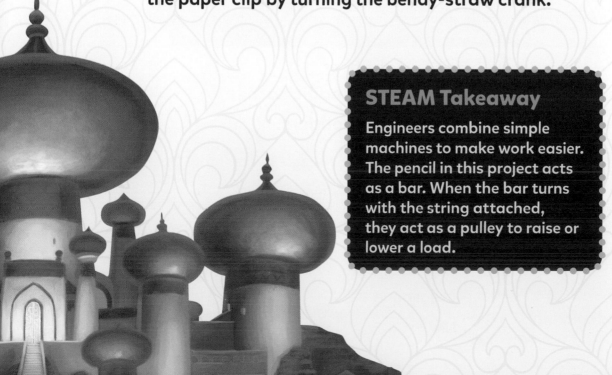

STEAM Takeaway

Engineers combine simple machines to make work easier. The pencil in this project acts as a bar. When the bar turns with the string attached, they act as a pulley to raise or lower a load.

Jar of Molten Lava

Aladdin and Abu take a wild ride on a magic carpet to escape molten lava in the Cave of Wonders. Create your own bubbling molten lava.

Materials
- pint-size clear mason jar
- water
- red food coloring
- vegetable oil
- flashlight
- teaspoon
- salt

1. Fill about three-quarters of the mason jar with water. Add a few drops of red food coloring. Gently swirl the jar to mix the coloring.

2. Add vegetable oil to the water until the liquid gets to within about an inch (2.5 cm) of the top of the jar. Wait a few moments as the oil and water separate.

3. Place a flashlight behind the jar, and shine its light into the oil and water.

4. Pour 3 teaspoons of salt into the jar, and watch the liquid bubble like molten lava.

5. When the bubbles stop, add more salt to see them again.

STEAM Takeaway

Oil is lighter than water, so it floats. Salt is heavier than oil and water. When you pour salt into the mixture, it sinks and gets coated in oil. Some of the salt dissolves when it reaches the water, and the oil coating rises in bubbles to the surface.

Release Genie

Genie appears when someone rubs his lamp.
You can release a surprise from a bottle too.

Materials

- empty plastic water bottle
- plastic tray (optional)
- kitchen funnel
- ¼ cup hydrogen peroxide
- liquid dish soap
- blue food coloring
- small bowl
- ¼-ounce (7 g) packet dry yeast
- ¼ cup warm water
- spoon

1. Set the water bottle in an empty sink or on a plastic tray. With an adult's help, use the kitchen funnel to carefully add the hydrogen peroxide to the bottle.

2. Squeeze about a teaspoon of dish soap into the bottle. Add 4 to 5 drops of blue food coloring. Gently swirl the bottle to mix the solution.

3. In a separate bowl, mix the dry yeast into the warm water. Gently stir the solution with the spoon.

4. Use the kitchen funnel to add the yeast and water solution to the bottle in the sink or on the tray.

5. Move the funnel away, and watch the solution release from the bottle like Genie would!

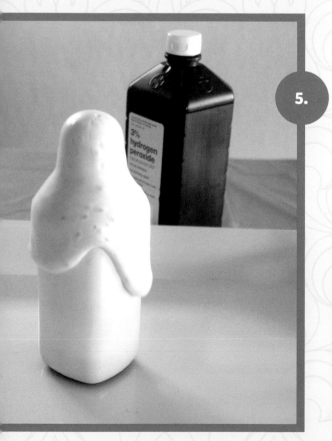

STEAM Takeaway

Mixing yeast and hydrogen peroxide starts a fast-moving chemical reaction. The yeast breaks down hydrogen peroxide to form oxygen and water. The oxygen combines with the dish soap to form bubbles.

Sultan Puppet

Jafar attaches strings to the Sultan to control him like a puppet. Design a Sultan puppet that moves when you pull its strings.

Materials
- school glue
- 2 craft sticks
- hole punch
- toilet paper cardboard tube
- ruler
- scissors
- twine
- yarn
- card stock paper or index card
- markers
- cotton ball

1. Glue 2 craft sticks together in a plus sign. Allow the glue to dry. This will be the handle to control the puppet.

2. Punch 2 holes near one end of the toilet paper tube. The holes should be on opposite sides of the tube. Then do the same on the other end of the tube. Punch another hole near the middle of the tube on a side that doesn't already have a hole.

3. Cut 2 (10-inch, or 25 cm) pieces of twine. Thread a twine piece through the holes at the top of the tube for arms. Let the arms stick out from the tube. Thread the other twine piece through the bottom holes for legs. Tie a knot at both ends of the strings.

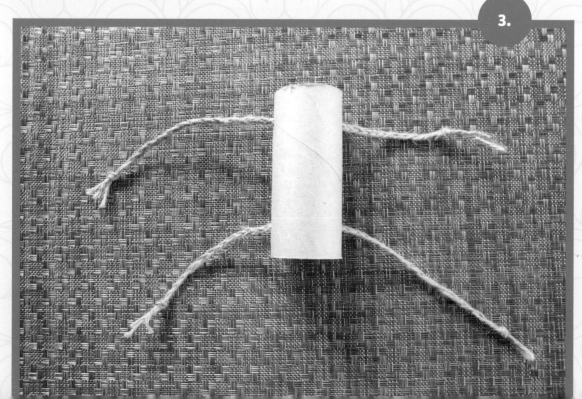

4. Cut 4 (12-inch, or 30 cm) pieces of yarn. Tie the pieces onto the ends of the handle you made in step 1. Attach the yarn pieces so that most of the yarn hangs down.

5. Tie the ends of 2 yarn pieces that are hanging from the same craft stick to the ends of the twine arms. Tie a yarn piece to one of the twine legs.

6. Thread the final yarn piece through the hole on the back of the tube. Make a loop, and tie the yarn in a knot.

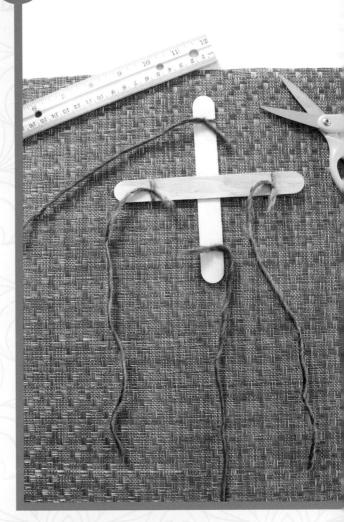

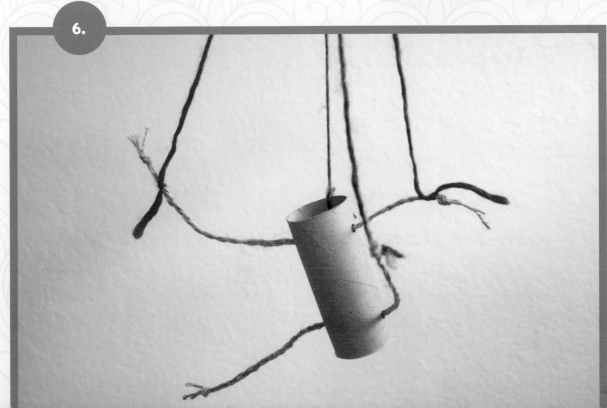

7. On the card stock paper or index card, draw and color the Sultan's head and hat. Cut out the head and hat. Then glue the head and hat to the top front of the puppet.

8. Gently stretch a cotton ball until it looks like the Sultan's fluffy beard. Glue the beard to the bottom of the puppet's head.

9. Move the craft-stick handle to control your puppet!

7.

STEAM Takeaway

A marionette is a puppet that a puppeteer usually controls from above with strings or wires. People around the world have created marionettes for thousands of years. The earliest marionettes were often made of clay or wood and were controlled with strings or wooden rods.

Sands of Time Hourglass

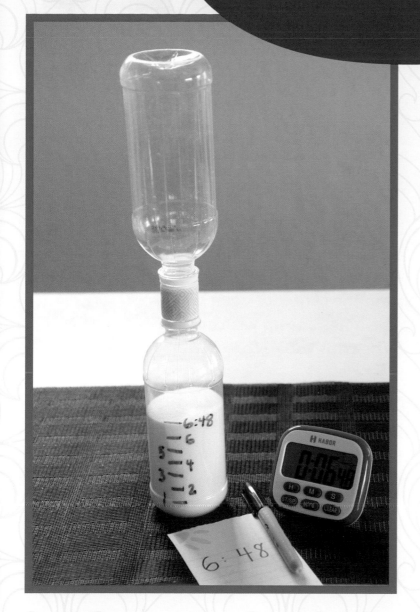

Jafar uses the Sands of Time hourglass for his evil plans. Create an hourglass to keep track of time.

Materials
- 2 matching clear plastic water bottles with caps
- pushpin
- kitchen skewer or large nail
- kitchen funnel
- salt or sand
- masking tape
- timer
- marker

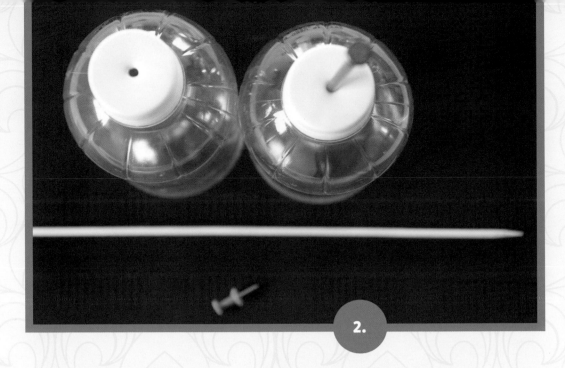

2.

1. Ask an adult to poke a hole in the center of each bottle cap with the pushpin. Be sure the holes line up with each other. You can check by stacking the caps top to top.

2. Enlarge the holes by inserting the skewer or nail and moving it around.

3. Use the kitchen funnel to fill one bottle with salt or sand. Fill about two-thirds of the bottle.

4. Tighten the caps on both bottles. Place the empty bottle upside down on top of the other bottle.

3.

5. Tightly wrap masking tape around the caps to attach the bottles to each other.

6. Holding the taped middle, carefully turn the hourglass upside down and start the timer.

7. Watch the timer and the sand. At the end of each minute, use the marker to make a line on the bottle showing how deep the sand is.

8. Keep watching until all the sand has fallen into the bottom bottle. Make a final line on the bottle at the top of the sand. Next to the line, write how long it took all the sand to fall. Now you can use your hourglass to keep time!

Magnetic Carpet Ride

Jasmine and Aladdin fly on a magic carpet over Agrabah. You can make a magnetic carpet that is almost as magical.

Materials
- masking tape
- 2 hobby magnets
- small piece of fabric such as felt
- scissors
- empty cereal box

1. With a small piece of rolled-up masking tape, attach a magnet to the center of the fabric.

2. Cut a piece of cardboard from the cereal box. Make sure the cutout cardboard is larger than the piece of fabric.

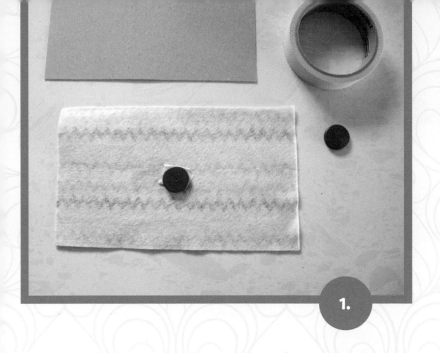

1.

3. Place the fabric on top of the cardboard. The magnet should be between the cardboard and the fabric.

4. Hold the cardboard by its edge. With your other hand, hold the second magnet under the cardboard. Move the second magnet closer to the magnet beneath the carpet until they attract each other. If they push away instead, flip over the magnet in your hand and try again. The cardboard will be sandwiched between the magnets.

5. Slide the lower magnet around the cardboard. Watch the magnetic carpet move without touching it!

5.

STEAM Takeaway

Magnets are surrounded by invisible magnetic fields. The fields attract or push away from one another depending on a magnet's poles. A magnet's north pole attracts another magnet's south pole. Two north poles or two south poles push away from each other.

Glossary

bar: a long and narrow piece of wood or metal used to do a job

chemical reaction: when two or more chemicals interact to create a new substance

hourglass: a timekeeping tool that allows sand to pass from an upper chamber to a lower chamber in a certain amount of time

marionette: a puppet controlled with strings

molten: melted by heat into a liquid

puppeteer: a person who controls a puppet

solution: liquid mixed with one or more substances

sultan: a king

zip line: a cable that people ride down a slope

To Learn More

Books

Ahrens, Niki. *Moana Idea Lab*. Minneapolis: Lerner Publications, 2020.
Explore the world of Moana through science, technology, engineering, art, and math projects.

Heinecke, Liz Lee. *STEAM Lab for Kids: 52 Creative Hands-On Projects for Exploring Science, Technology, Engineering, Art, and Math*. Beverly, MA: Quarry Books, 2018.
Create and learn with hands-on STEAM projects.

Websites

8 Things You Didn't Know about *Aladdin*
https://ohmy.disney.com/movies/2015/10/13/8-things-you-didnt-know-about-aladdin/
See images and learn more about the movie *Aladdin*.

The Essential List of *Aladdin* Quotes
https://ohmy.disney.com/quotes/2018/05/25/aladdin-quotes/
Read fun quotes from your favorite *Aladdin* characters.

Index

Photo Acknowledgments

Additional image credits: Belozersky/Shutterstock.com (beaker); E_K/ Shutterstock.com (gears); Aksenova Natalya/Shutterstock.com, p. 6 (glue); Olga Kovalenko/Shutterstock.com, p. 6 (scissors); Lyudmila Suvorova/Shutterstock.com, p. 7 (paper); SJ Travel Photo and Video/ Shutterstock.com, p. 7 (paints).